Merseyside Legacy
of
Jürgen Klopp

(2015-2024)

Impact and Tactical Brilliance of Klopp in Reshaping Liverpool Football Club's Game in the Modern Era and Highlights of Emotional Moments at Anfield

Michael L. Watson

Dedication

To the unwavering support and boundless love of my parents who have been the steadfast pillars upon which my dreams have soared. Your encouragement and belief in my journey have been the driving force behind every word penned in this book.

To my well-wishers, whose optimism and cheering voices have echoed in the background of my writing days, providing the motivation needed to overcome challenges and embrace triumphs. Your belief in my creative endeavors has been a source of inspiration that I carry with pride.

And, above all, to the Almighty, the Divine orchestrator of destinies, who granted me the gift of creativity and the opportunity to weave stories. In moments of solitude and uncertainty, your guidance has been my compass, steering me through the labyrinth of imagination.

May the words within these pages be a humble offering of gratitude to those whose love and blessings have illuminated my path. This book is dedicated to the enduring spirits of family, friendship, and the Divine forces that shape our narratives.

Table of Contents

Introduction

Jürgen Klopp's Impact on Liverpool: A Managerial Legacy Unveiled

In the annals of football history, certain managerial reigns shine brightly, leaving an indelible mark on the clubs they led. Among these luminaries, Jürgen Klopp's time at Liverpool stands out as a saga of triumph, transformation, and unwavering commitment. This introduction aims to provide a brief overview of Klopp's impact on Liverpool, underscoring the profound significance of his managerial tenure.

When Klopp assumed the reins at Liverpool in October 2015, the club was at a crossroads. Enduring a period of relative instability, the Reds were yearning for a leader who could revive their former glories. Klopp, renowned for his dynamic approach and charismatic demeanor, proved to be the catalyst that Liverpool needed. His appointment signaled the beginning of a new era, characterized by spirited football, tactical ingenuity, and a genuine connection with the supporters.

The significance of Klopp's arrival went beyond the pitch; it was a marriage of football philosophy and club ethos. Liverpool, a club steeped in history and tradition, found a kindred spirit in Klopp. His passion for the game mirrored the fervor of the Anfield faithful, creating an instant resonance. The charismatic German manager quickly became a symbol of hope and rejuvenation, breathing life into the storied club.

One of the key elements that define Klopp's impact is his ability to instill a sense of belief in both players and fans alike. Liverpool, under his guidance, transcended the boundaries of expectation, setting audacious goals and achieving them. From the electrifying nights at Anfield to memorable European triumphs, Klopp's tenure witnessed a resurgence that captivated the footballing world.

The Premier League title drought that had plagued Liverpool for three decades came to a triumphant end under Klopp's stewardship. The 2019-2020 season marked a historic achievement as Liverpool clinched the league title, a feat that resonated deeply with the passionate supporters who had waited patiently for this moment. Klopp's tears of joy and unbridled celebrations mirrored the collective emotions of a fanbase that had endured the highs and lows of the journey.

Beyond the silverware, Klopp's impact extended to the very fabric of the club. He not only molded a formidable team but fostered a sense of camaraderie and unity. The "gegenpressing" style of play became synonymous with Liverpool's identity, reflecting Klopp's tactical acumen and commitment to entertaining football. The team's relentless work ethic, epitomized by high-intensity pressing and swift counter-attacks, was a testament to Klopp's coaching philosophy.

In the context of Liverpool's rich history, Klopp's tenure can be seen as a transformative chapter. He took the helm at a time when the club needed not just a manager but a visionary leader. His charisma, expressed through touchline exuberance and heartfelt interactions with players, resonated far beyond the confines of the pitch. Anfield became a fortress once again, and Liverpool's distinctive anthem, "You'll Never Walk Alone," echoed with newfound vigor.

Chapter One: The Pre-Klopp Era: Liverpool's Odyssey Before the German Maestro

Before Jürgen Klopp stepped into the hallowed halls of Anfield, Liverpool Football Club navigated a complex and often tumultuous landscape. Understanding the historical context of the club before Klopp's arrival unveils a narrative marked by both glorious triumphs and challenging tribulations.

The Twilight Years of Roy Hodgson and Transition

As Klopp took charge in October 2015, Liverpool was emerging from a period of managerial transitions, where the tenure of Roy Hodgson cast a shadow over Anfield. Hodgson's time at Liverpool, from July 2010 to January 2011, was marked by a lack of cohesion on the pitch and strained relations with the fanbase. The club, accustomed to European success and domestic dominance, found itself in a state of flux. Kenny Dalglish's return in January 2011 injected a sense of nostalgia and hope. Yet, despite winning the League Cup in the 2011-2012 season, Liverpool struggled to recapture the glory days of the past. The club was grappling with a changing landscape in English football, where financial disparities and the rise of dominant rivals added complexity to their quest for supremacy.

Brendan Rodgers and the Near Miss of 2013-2014

Brendan Rodgers assumed the managerial reins in June 2012, bringing with him a commitment to stylish and attacking football. The 2013-2014 season emerged as a tantalizing chapter in Liverpool's recent history. Led by the remarkable strike partnership of Luis Suárez and Daniel Sturridge, the Reds played scintillating football, coming agonizingly close to clinching the Premier League title.

However, the slip against Chelsea and the subsequent narrow miss of the title highlighted the fragility of Liverpool's squad and the need for sustained excellence. The departure of Suárez to Barcelona in the summer of 2014 added to the challenges, leaving a void that proved challenging to fill.

The Dearth of European Football

One of the stark contrasts before Klopp's era was Liverpool's absence from European competitions. While the club had a storied history in European football, the absence of consistent Champions League football became a notable feature. This not only impacted the club's financial standing but also hindered their ability to attract top-tier talent.

Liverpool was navigating the Premier League with sporadic success, but the absence from the grand stage of European competitions underscored a period of rebuilding and reassessment. The years leading up to Klopp's appointment were characterized by a hunger for stability and a return to the upper echelons of both domestic and European football.

A Club in Search of Identity

The pre-Klopp era saw Liverpool grappling with questions of identity and playing philosophy. While the club's heritage was rich with attacking football and memorable European nights, there was a sense that Liverpool needed a visionary leader to instill a clear identity. The Anfield faithful yearned for a manager who could not only bring success on the pitch but also revive the ethos that defined Liverpool's golden eras.

In essence, the state of Liverpool before Klopp's arrival was one of transition, unfulfilled promise, and a hunger for renewed glory. The club had a proud history, but recent years had tested the resilience of both players and supporters. The appointment of Jürgen Klopp would prove to be the catalyst that transformed this narrative, laying the foundation for a remarkable chapter in Liverpool's storied history.

Challenges Before Klopp: A Club in Transition

Before the arrival of Jürgen Klopp, Liverpool Football Club found itself grappling with a myriad of challenges that tested the resilience of both players and supporters. These challenges, in turn, set the stage for Klopp's transformative impact on the club.

Financial Constraints and Competing in the Premier League

Liverpool's financial landscape was undergoing shifts, with the club facing challenges in competing with the financial might of certain Premier League rivals. The post-2008 economic landscape of football saw the emergence of clubs with substantial financial backing, creating a competitive imbalance. Liverpool, while historically successful, had to navigate these financial constraints in assembling a squad capable of challenging for top honors.

The financial limitations impacted the club's ability to attract and retain marquee players. It also influenced transfer strategies, leading to a reliance on scouting and development. This period saw Liverpool in a constant struggle to find the right balance between financial prudence and on-field success.

Defensive Fragility and Squad Depth

On the pitch, one of Liverpool's significant challenges was defensive fragility. The team struggled with consistency at the back, conceding goals that hindered their progress in both domestic and European competitions. The lack of a solid defensive foundation meant that even prolific attacking displays were undermined by vulnerabilities at the back.

Furthermore, squad depth became a pressing issue. Injuries to key players often exposed the limitations of the squad, especially during congested fixture schedules. Liverpool needed a manager who could not only address defensive frailties but also build a squad capable of sustained competitiveness across various competitions.

Managerial Instability

The revolving door of managerial changes also posed a challenge. In the post-Rafael Benítez era, Liverpool went through several managerial appointments, each with varying degrees of success. This lack of stability at the managerial helm contributed to a sense of uncertainty within the club. Players had to adapt to different tactical philosophies and managerial styles, hindering the establishment of a cohesive team identity.

Reviving European Ambitions

Liverpool's absence from consistent Champions League football was a stark challenge. The club's storied history in European competitions was marked by memorable triumphs, but recent years saw a lapse in regular participation at the highest level. The quest to revive European ambitions and secure a place among the continent's elite became a pressing objective.

Achievements in the Face of Adversity

Amidst these challenges, Liverpool still managed notable achievements. The 2011-2012 League Cup triumph under

Kenny Dalglish provided a moment of celebration, and the scintillating football played during Brendan Rodgers' tenure showcased the club's attacking prowess. Despite the hurdles, there were glimpses of the Liverpool spirit that craved success.

The challenges outlined above, while formidable, laid the groundwork for the narrative of Jürgen Klopp's tenure. The German manager, known for his ability to build resilient teams and inspire collective efforts, would step into a scenario where overcoming challenges was not just a goal but a necessity.

As we transition into the Klopp era in subsequent sections, it's crucial to recognize the adversities that paved the way for Klopp's transformative impact.

The challenges Liverpool faced were not insurmountable; they were the raw material that Klopp would shape into the foundation of a new, dynamic era for Liverpool Football Club.

Edit extensively

Chapter Two: Jürgen Klopp: Architect of Glory - A Preamble to the Liverpool Legacy

Before the charismatic German maestro, Jürgen Klopp, orchestrated the symphony of success at Liverpool, his managerial journey unfolded across various clubs in Germany, laying the groundwork for the dynamic style and spirited ethos that would become synonymous with his name.

Mainz 05: Cultivating the Seeds of Success (2001-2008)

Jürgen Klopp's managerial journey took its formative steps at Mainz 05, a club in the lower tiers of German football, where he would sow the seeds of his innovative footballing philosophy. Appointed in February 2001, Klopp faced the challenge of transforming a modest club into a force to be reckoned with.

Key Roles at Mainz 05

Klopp's initial role at Mainz 05 was not just about managing a football team; it was about reshaping the entire culture of the club. He assumed the responsibilities of both coach and manager, overseeing not only the first team but also playing a pivotal role in shaping the club's overall footballing vision.

One of Klopp's key contributions was introducing the concept of gegenpressing, an aggressive and immediate pressing strategy designed to win the ball back as quickly as possible after losing possession. This tactical innovation laid the foundation for the high-intensity, dynamic style that would become a hallmark of Klopp's managerial career.

Accomplishments at Mainz 05

Under Klopp's guidance, Mainz experienced unprecedented success. The pinnacle of his tenure came in the 2003-2004 season when Mainz secured promotion to the Bundesliga for the first time in the club's history. This achievement was not just a promotion; it was a testament to Klopp's ability to elevate a club with limited resources to a higher echelon of German football.

Klopp's impact went beyond on-field success; he fostered a sense of belief and unity within the club. The charismatic manager's ability to connect with players and fans alike created an atmosphere of enthusiasm and optimism. Even though Mainz faced relegation in the subsequent Bundesliga season, Klopp had laid the groundwork for a footballing philosophy that would resonate far beyond his time at the club.

Borussia Dortmund: The Glory Years (2008-2015)

The next chapter of Klopp's managerial odyssey saw him take charge of Borussia Dortmund in May 2008. It was here that Klopp's managerial prowess reached its zenith, as he transformed

Dortmund into one of the most exciting and successful teams in European football.

Key Roles at Borussia Dortmund

At Dortmund, Klopp assumed the role of head coach, a position that allowed him greater influence over the first team's affairs. His impact extended to player recruitment and overall footballing strategy. Klopp not only focused on assembling a talented squad but also on nurturing young talents through the club's renowned youth academy.

Klopp's influence at Dortmund went beyond traditional coaching responsibilities; he became a charismatic leader who instilled a sense of camaraderie and purpose within the squad. His ability to create a collective identity, where players bought into a shared vision, became a defining characteristic of his managerial style.

Accomplishments at Borussia Dortmund

Under Klopp's tutelage, Borussia Dortmund experienced a period of unparalleled success. The 2010-2011 and 2011-2012 seasons marked a historic achievement as Dortmund clinched back-to-back Bundesliga titles. The manner in which Dortmund secured these titles, playing an exhilarating brand of attacking football, captivated football enthusiasts worldwide.

The pinnacle of Klopp's time at Dortmund was the run to the UEFA Champions League final in the 2012-2013 season. Although Dortmund fell short against Bayern Munich in the final, the journey showcased Klopp's ability to compete at the highest echelons of European football.

Beyond domestic success, Klopp's Dortmund left an indelible mark on the footballing landscape. His gegenpressing tactics became synonymous with the team's identity. Players like Robert Lewandowski, Marco Reus, and Mats Hummels thrived under Klopp's guidance, elevating their performances to new heights.

The charismatic manager's achievements extended to the DFB-Pokal, where Dortmund secured victories in the competition during Klopp's tenure. The collective jubilation and celebrations at the

Westfalenstadion were not just about winning titles; they were about a resurgence of a footballing ethos that resonated with fans on a visceral level.

Transitioning to Liverpool (2015)

Jürgen Klopp's key roles and accomplishments at Mainz 05 and Borussia Dortmund form the bedrock of his managerial legacy. The success he achieved, coupled with the tactical innovations and the emotional resonance he established at these clubs, set the stage for the next chapter in Klopp's managerial journey: the transformative era at Liverpool. As we transition to Klopp's impact on Liverpool, it's crucial to recognize how his experiences at Mainz and Dortmund shaped not only his managerial philosophy but also the expectations that would surround him as he stepped onto the Anfield stage.

In October 2015, Liverpool came calling, seeking a manager who could inject new life into the club. Jürgen Klopp's arrival on Merseyside was met with anticipation and excitement. His managerial pedigree and the success he achieved in Germany made him a sought-after figure, and Liverpool fans were eager to witness the Klopp effect.

The transition from Dortmund to Liverpool was not just a change of clubs for Klopp; it was a cultural shift. The expectations and traditions of Liverpool, a club with a storied history, added a new layer of complexity to Klopp's managerial journey. Yet, it was precisely this challenge that fueled Klopp's ambition.

Striking a Chord: Klopp's Early Impact at Liverpool

Klopp's influence at Liverpool was evident from the outset. His charismatic personality, combined with a clear footballing philosophy, resonated with players and fans alike. The gegenpressing style, honed in Germany, found a new home at Anfield. Klopp's emphasis on unity, hard work, and a never-say-die attitude began to redefine the identity of Liverpool Football Club.

In his first full season (2016-2017), Klopp led Liverpool back to the Champions League, showcasing the early signs of a reinvigorated force. The exhilarating attacking displays, coupled with memorable European nights, signaled a promising future under Klopp's stewardship.

Tactical Ingenuity and Emotional Resonance

Klopp's managerial journey isn't merely a chronicle of victories and titles; it's a narrative woven with tactical ingenuity and emotional resonance. His ability to mold teams into cohesive, attacking units reflects a deep understanding of the beautiful game. The gegenpressing style, refined at Mainz and perfected at Dortmund, became a tactical trademark that Liverpool embraced.

Beyond tactics, Klopp's charisma and emotional connection with players stand out. His knack for nurturing young talents and extracting the best from experienced campaigners became a hallmark of his managerial approach. The famous 'heavy metal' football, as Klopp described his high-octane style, wasn't just a tactical strategy; it was a reflection of his passion and commitment to entertaining the fans.

Jürgen Klopp's managerial journey before Liverpool serves as a prologue to the golden era he would orchestrate on the Anfield stage. From the modest beginnings at Mainz to the glory-laden years at Borussia Dortmund, Klopp honed his craft, evolving into a manager capable of transforming clubs and leaving an indelible mark.

As we delve deeper into Klopp's impact at Liverpool in subsequent sections, it's crucial to appreciate the layers of experience, tactical innovation, and emotional resonance that define his managerial journey. Klopp's arrival at Liverpool wasn't just a change of personnel; it was a convergence of footballing philosophies, cultural shifts, and a shared vision for success. The chapters that follow will unravel the nuances of Klopp's time at Liverpool, a saga that transcends the boundaries of victories and trophies to encompass the very essence of the beautiful game.

Chapter Three: The Marriage of Klopp and Liverpool: A Union Forged in Red

The appointment of Jürgen Klopp as the manager of Liverpool Football Club in October 2015 marked the beginning of a transformative journey, a union that would redefine the trajectory of the club and etch Klopp's name in Anfield folklore. This section delves into the intricacies of Klopp's arrival, the initial challenges faced, and the adjustments made as the charismatic German sought to breathe new life into one of England's most storied football institutions.

The Arrival: October 2015

In the fall of 2015, Liverpool found itself at a crossroads. The departure of

Brendan Rodgers, the charismatic Northern Irishman who had come close to securing the Premier League title in the 2013-2014 season, left a void that needed filling. Liverpool's ownership, Fenway Sports Group, sought a manager who could not only build on the positive aspects of Rodgers' tenure but also inject a fresh impetus into the club's ambitions.

Enter Jürgen Klopp, the enigmatic German whose reputation for dynamic football, infectious passion, and charismatic touchline presence had been forged through successful stints at Mainz 05 and Borussia Dortmund. Klopp, known for his gegenpressing style and ability to forge a strong bond with both players and fans, emerged as the frontrunner for the Anfield hot seat.

On October 8, 2015, the announcement was made, and Anfield welcomed Klopp with open arms. The charismatic manager's infectious smile and confident demeanor immediately resonated with the Liverpool faithful. It wasn't just a managerial appointment; it was a cultural shift, a marriage of a club yearning for success and a manager hungry to leave an indelible mark.

The First Impressions: A Wave of Enthusiasm

Klopp's first interactions with the media and fans set the tone for what was to come. His charismatic press conferences, sprinkled with humor and passion, endeared him to Liverpool supporters. The famous "doubters to believers" mantra echoed through Anfield, encapsulating Klopp's belief in transforming the mindset and expectations surrounding the club.

Fans, still savoring the memories of Istanbul and the glory days under managers like Bill Shankly and Bob Paisley, found in Klopp a leader who not only understood the ethos of Liverpool but was also determined to revive it. The atmosphere at Anfield became electric, infused with a renewed sense of optimism and anticipation for the Klopp era.

Initial Challenges: Navigating Transition and Expectations

Despite the wave of enthusiasm, Klopp faced immediate challenges. He inherited a squad that, while talented, lacked consistency and defensive solidity. The transition from Brendan Rodgers' possession-based style to Klopp's gegenpressing demanded adjustments, both in terms of player mindset and tactical execution.

Adapting the Squad to Gegenpressing:

Gegenpressing, a tactical approach focused on pressing the opposition intensely immediately after losing possession, was a fundamental tenet of Klopp's footballing philosophy. The players had to adapt to the demands of this high-energy system, requiring not only physical fitness but also a mental shift in their approach to the game.

Injuries and Squad Depth:

Injuries further complicated the early stages of Klopp's tenure. Key players faced spells on the sidelines, exposing the lack of depth in certain positions. Klopp had to navigate congested fixture schedules with a squad that was often stretched thin, requiring strategic rotations and reliance on younger talents.

Striking a Balance:

Finding the right balance between defensive solidity and attacking flair was a delicate task. Klopp's commitment to entertaining football and high-scoring encounters sometimes left the defense vulnerable. Striking the right balance between flair and resilience became a crucial aspect of Liverpool's evolution under Klopp.

Adjustments and Early Signs of Progress

As challenges mounted, Klopp's adaptability and strategic acumen became apparent. The early signs of progress were seen in the team's performances and glimpses of the gegenpressing style that would come to define Klopp's Liverpool.

Emphasis on Team Unity:

Klopp's emphasis on team unity was a catalyst for change. He fostered a sense of camaraderie and collective responsibility that transcended individual brilliance. The famous 'gegenpressing orchestra' required every player to contribute, fostering a sense of togetherness that became a hallmark of Klopp's teams.

Strategic Signings:

Klopp wasted no time in imprinting his vision on the squad. Strategic signings, such as the acquisition of players like Sadio Mané and Joel Matip, injected pace and defensive solidity into the team. These signings laid the foundation for a squad that could execute Klopp's tactical blueprint effectively.

Cup Runs and European Nights:

Liverpool's journey in domestic cup competitions and memorable European nights provided glimpses of Klopp's impact. Victories over the likes of

Manchester United and Borussia Dortmund in the Europa League showcased the resilience and belief instilled by the German manager.

The Road Ahead: Building for the Future

The initial challenges and adjustments were part of a larger process of rebuilding. Klopp's vision extended beyond immediate success; he aimed to lay the foundations for sustained excellence. The marriage between Klopp and Liverpool was evolving, with each challenge met and overcome contributing to the narrative of a club in transition.

As Klopp steered Liverpool through the challenges of the 2015-2016 season, the seeds of transformation were being planted. The journey was one of evolution, with Klopp as the orchestrator, guiding Liverpool through the twists and turns that would lead to a brighter, more triumphant future.

The marriage of Jürgen Klopp and Liverpool in October 2015 was more than a managerial appointment; it was the convergence of footballing philosophies, a shared vision, and the collective aspirations of a club and its supporters. The initial challenges and adjustments were integral chapters in the unfolding narrative of Klopp's Liverpool.

It is crucial to remember the early days – a period where Klopp laid the groundwork for a renaissance, where challenges were met with resilience, and adjustments paved the way for a transformation that would resonate far beyond the touchline at Anfield. The marriage between Klopp and Liverpool was not just a union of coach and club; it was a fusion of passion, ambition, and the unwavering belief that glory awaited on the horizon.

Chapter Four: Building the Gegenpressing Legacy: Klopp's Tactical Symphony

Klopp's Tactical Philosophy and Implementation of Gegenpressing

Jürgen Klopp's tactical philosophy is synonymous with the term "gegenpressing," a strategic approach that not only defines his teams but has also left an indelible mark on modern football. Gegenpressing, which translates to "counter-pressing" in German, is not just a tactical system; it's a manifestation of Klopp's footballing ideology and his emphasis on collective, high-intensity play.

High-Intensity Pressing:

At its core, gegenpressing is about winning the ball back immediately after losing possession. Klopp's teams are characterized by an aggressive and coordinated pressing style that aims to disrupt the opponent's build-up play and regain control of the ball as quickly as possible. This high-intensity pressing isn't just a defensive strategy; it's a means to initiate attacks and maintain a relentless tempo throughout the match.

Collective Effort:

What sets Klopp's gegenpressing apart is the emphasis on collective effort. Every player, regardless of position, is involved in pressing and winning the ball back. It requires not just physical fitness but also a deep understanding of positional play and a shared commitment to the team's defensive and offensive transitions.

Transition from Defense to Attack:
Gegenpressing is not merely a defensive strategy. It serves as a powerful tool for transitioning from defense to attack. By winning the ball back quickly, Klopp's teams catch opponents off guard, exploiting the moment of disorganization. This transition is characterized by rapid ball circulation, quick forward passes, and exploiting spaces left open by the retreating opposition.

Evolution of Playing Style and Strategies

As Klopp's managerial journey progressed, so did the evolution of his playing style and strategic approach. Gegenpressing remained a constant, but Klopp showcased his adaptability by incorporating new elements and strategies to keep his teams unpredictable and dynamic.

Development of Midfield Pressing:

While gegenpressing initially focused on pressing in the opponent's defensive third, Klopp's tactical evolution saw the incorporation of midfield pressing. This involved intensifying the press higher up the pitch, denying opponents time and space to build their attacks. The midfield press became a key element in disrupting the rhythm of opposition play.

Flexibility in Formation:

Klopp demonstrated tactical flexibility by not being wedded to a specific formation. While he often employed a 4-3-3 or 4-2-3-1 formation, he adapted based on the strengths of his squad and the specific requirements of a match. This flexibility allowed Liverpool to seamlessly switch between different formations, keeping opponents guessing.

Incorporation of Vertical Passing:

As Klopp's teams matured, there was a noticeable emphasis on vertical passing. Gegenpressing wasn't just about regaining possession; it was about making progressive passes into dangerous areas. The ability to play incisive, vertical passes allowed Klopp's teams to exploit spaces and create goal-scoring opportunities.

Set-Piece Mastery:

In addition to open play, Klopp's teams became proficient in set-piece situations. Whether defending or attacking set-pieces, there was a strategic organization and emphasis on exploiting set-piece opportunities. This attention to detail contributed to Liverpool's effectiveness in both defensive solidity and offensive prowess from dead-ball situations.

Adaptation to Squad Dynamics:

One of Klopp's strengths is his ability to adapt his tactics to suit the strengths of his squad. The evolution of playing style wasn't a rigid adherence to a predefined system but a dynamic process that considered the players at his disposal. The recruitment of players who fit into the gegenpressing philosophy ensured a seamless integration of new talents.

Legacy and Impact

Klopp's gegenpressing legacy isn't just about tactical innovations on the pitch; it's about the impact it has had on footballing culture. Gegenpressing became a buzzword in football discussions, and many managers sought to replicate its success. The influence extended beyond Klopp's own teams to inspire a broader shift in footballing philosophies.

Inspiring a Gegenpressing Trend:
The success of Klopp's gegenpressing at Mainz, Borussia Dortmund, and Liverpool triggered a trend across European football. Many managers,

both seasoned and emerging, incorporated elements of gegenpressing into their tactical setups. The philosophy of immediate ball recovery after losing possession became a hallmark of progressive and dynamic teams.

Gegenpressing's Effect on Fan Engagement:

Beyond its impact on the pitch, gegenpressing transformed the fan experience. The high-octane, exhilarating style of play resonated with supporters, creating an emotional connection. The sight of players relentlessly pressing and chasing every ball became a visual representation of the commitment and passion that fans cherish.

Influence on English Football:

Klopp's arrival in the Premier League with Liverpool brought gegenpressing to the forefront of English football. The intense, fast-paced nature of the Premier League suited Klopp's style, and other clubs began to adjust their strategies to cope with or emulate the gegenpressing approach. The tactical landscape of English football underwent a transformation with Klopp at the helm.

European Success and Global Recognition:

Klopp's gegenpressing philosophy bore fruit on the grandest stages of European football. The journey to the UEFA Champions League final in 2018 and the triumph in 2019 showcased the effectiveness of gegenpressing against elite opponents. The global recognition and acclaim received by Klopp and his teams further solidified gegenpressing as a tactical legacy with a lasting imprint.

The legacy of Jürgen Klopp's gegenpressing is a testament to the fusion of tactical innovation, collective effort, and a relentless pursuit of success. What began as a strategic approach evolved into a cultural phenomenon that resonated across footballing landscapes. Klopp's gegenpressing legacy isn't just about winning matches; it's about transforming the way the beautiful game is played, experienced, and celebrated. As we delve deeper into the subsequent sections, exploring the triumphs and nuances of Klopp's tenure, it's crucial to recognize how gegenpressing became more than a tactical philosophy – it became a symphony, with Klopp as the conductor orchestrating success, passion, and a footballing revolution.

Chapter Five: Triumphs and Trophies: Jürgen Klopp's Era of Glory

The Road to Triumph: Highlights of Major Achievements

Jürgen Klopp's tenure at Liverpool has been nothing short of extraordinary, characterized by a cascade of triumphs and the hoisting of prestigious trophies that have eluded the club for years. From the unforgettable nights in the UEFA Champions League to the crowning glory of a long-awaited Premier League title, Klopp's era is a testament to resilience, tactical brilliance, and a team ethos that resonated with fans worldwide.

UEFA Champions League Glory (2018-2019)

The pinnacle of Klopp's early success at Liverpool came in the 2018-2019 season, as the Reds embarked on a remarkable journey to claim their sixth UEFA Champions League title. The campaign was marked by dramatic comebacks, stunning performances, and an unwavering belief that characterized Klopp's ethos.

Group Stage Drama:

Liverpool navigated a challenging group stage that included Paris Saint-Germain, Napoli, and Red Star Belgrade. A crucial away win against PSG set the tone for a resilient campaign, with late goals and moments of individual brilliance becoming synonymous with Liverpool's European exploits.

Quarterfinal Classic vs. Barcelona: The quarterfinal tie against Barcelona is etched into football folklore. Trailing 3-0 from the first leg, Liverpool orchestrated a historic comeback at Anfield, winning 4-0 in one of the most memorable European nights. Divock Origi and Georginio Wijnaldum became unlikely heroes, and Trent Alexander-Arnold's quick corner kick that led to the decisive goal showcased Klopp's tactical ingenuity.

Final Triumph in Madrid:

Liverpool faced Tottenham Hotspur in the final in Madrid. Mohamed Salah's early penalty and Divock Origi's second-half strike secured a 2-0 victory, sealing Liverpool's sixth Champions League title. Klopp's ability to motivate and inspire his players, combined with a team that thrived under pressure, laid the foundation for a European triumph that resonated with fans worldwide.

Premier League Crown (2019-2020)

The 2019-2020 Premier League season saw Liverpool crowned champions of England after a 30-year wait. Klopp's relentless pursuit of excellence, coupled with a squad that epitomized his footballing philosophy, resulted in a title triumph that brought joy to the hearts of Liverpool supporters globally.

Dominance and Early Sealing of the Title:

Liverpool's dominance was evident from the early stages of the season. A 26-game unbeaten run included emphatic victories and moments of individual brilliance, notably from players like Sadio Mané, Mohamed Salah, and Virgil van Dijk. The Reds sealed the title with a record seven games to spare, a testament to their consistency and the tactical acumen instilled by Klopp.

Tactical Brilliance and Squad Depth:

Klopp's tactical brilliance was exemplified in Liverpool's playing style, characterized by high-pressing, dynamic attacking play, and defensive solidity. The squad's depth, with contributions from players like Divock Origi, Joe Gomez, and others, showcased Klopp's ability to nurture a cohesive unit that could withstand challenges and maintain performance levels throughout the season.

Joyous Celebrations and Emotional Redemption:

The joyous scenes that followed Liverpool's official confirmation as Premier League champions were symbolic of the emotional journey undertaken by the club. For Klopp, it was a moment of redemption and fulfillment, having come close in previous seasons. The outpouring of emotion, both from Klopp and the players, underlined the significance of the title triumph.

UEFA Super Cup and FIFA Club World Cup Success (2019)

In addition to domestic and continental triumphs, Liverpool secured further silverware in 2019 with victories in the UEFA Super Cup and the FIFA Club World Cup.

Super Cup Drama vs. Chelsea:

The UEFA Super Cup final against Chelsea went to extra time, with Liverpool emerging victorious in a thrilling encounter that ended 2-2 after regular time. The Reds secured a 5-4 win on penalties, showcasing their resilience and ability to prevail in high-stakes situations.

Club World Cup Triumph in Qatar:

Liverpool traveled to Qatar for the FIFA Club World Cup, where they faced strong opposition. Klopp's side overcame Monterrey in the semifinals before defeating Flamengo in the final with a goal from Roberto Firmino in extra time. The Club World Cup victory added a global dimension to Liverpool's success under Klopp.

Continued European Excellence (2019-2020 and 2020-2021)

Following their Champions League triumph, Liverpool continued to excel in European competitions. Although they faced challenges in the 2019-2020 season, including an early exit from the Champions League, they reached the quarterfinals of the competition in the 2020-2021 season. Klopp's ability to maintain a high level of performance in

Europe underscored Liverpool's status as a formidable force on the continental stage.

Emphasis on Team Unity and Player Development

Beyond the silverware, Klopp's era at Liverpool is characterized by a profound emphasis on team unity and player development. The cohesion and camaraderie within the squad are evident on and off the pitch, with players often expressing admiration for Klopp's man-management skills and the supportive environment he has fostered.

Nurturing Young Talent:

Klopp's commitment to nurturing young talent is exemplified by the emergence of players like Trent Alexander-Arnold and Curtis Jones. The academy has played a crucial role under Klopp, with young talents seamlessly integrating into the first team and contributing to the club's success.

Player Bond and Collective Celebrations:

The bond between Klopp and his players extends beyond the professional realm. Collective celebrations, be it on the training ground or during matches, reflect a sense of unity and shared joy. Klopp's ability to create a family-like atmosphere has been pivotal in the team's success.

Resilience and Mental Strength:

Klopp's emphasis on mental strength has been a cornerstone of Liverpool's triumphs. The ability to bounce back from setbacks, showcased in comebacks and late goals, reflects a mental resilience instilled by Klopp. The manager's motivational skills and positive reinforcement contribute to a winning mentality within the squad.

Fan Engagement and Global Impact

Klopp's charismatic personality and the entertaining style of play employed by Liverpool under his management have garnered immense fan engagement and support globally. The impact extends beyond the pitch, with Klopp becoming a symbol of the club's resurgence and an inspirational figure for fans around the world.

Cultural Impact of "Heavy Metal Football":

Klopp's energetic touchline presence and the dynamic style of play have earned Liverpool the moniker of playing "Heavy Metal Football." This cultural impact goes beyond victories, contributing to the club's identity and resonating with fans who appreciate the passion and intensity associated with Klopp's approach.

Global Liverpool Community:

Under Klopp, Liverpool has expanded its global community, with fans from various corners of the world uniting in their support for the club. The global appeal is not just about success on the pitch but also the values and ethos embodied by Klopp and the team.

Charitable Initiatives and Social Responsibility:

Klopp's involvement in charitable initiatives and social responsibility projects has further endeared him to fans. His advocacy for social causes, combined with the team's community engagement, reflects a commitment to making a positive impact beyond the realms of football.

Jürgen Klopp's era at Liverpool, marked by triumphs and trophies, is a rich tapestry woven with threads of passion, resilience, and unwavering belief. From the European glory of the Champions League to the domestic triumph in the Premier League, Klopp's impact extends beyond silverware. It's about the unity of a squad, the development of young talents, and the global community of fans brought together under the banner of Liverpool FC.

The triumphs and trophies are not just markers of success; they are chapters in a story that continues to unfold, with Klopp as the architect of a glorious era for Liverpool Football Club.

Chapter Six: Record-Breaking Stats: Jürgen Klopp's Managerial Mastery at Liverpool

Examination of Klopp's Managerial Records at Liverpool

Jürgen Klopp's managerial tenure at Liverpool has been defined not only by the silverware he has brought to Anfield but also by the record-breaking statistics and milestones achieved by his teams. From historic winning runs to defensive resilience, Klopp has guided Liverpool to new heights, setting benchmarks that showcase the excellence and consistency synonymous with his managerial philosophy.

Overall Managerial Record in Liverpool

Klopp boasts the highest win percentage among Liverpool managers with 50 or more games, standing at an impressive 60.7% across all competitions. Since Klopp's arrival, Liverpool's Premier League points total of 671 ranks second, trailing only Manchester City's 716, while Tottenham takes the third spot with 583 points. In the Premier League, Klopp shares the record for the longest winning streak – a remarkable 18 consecutive victories achieved between October 2019 and February 2020, tying with Guardiola's Manchester City. Furthermore, Klopp holds the second-longest unbeaten run in the Premier League, spanning 44 games from January 2019 to February 2020. This places him just behind Arsene Wenger's Arsenal, who achieved a longer unbeaten run between May 2003 and October 2004.

- **Total Matches:** Klopp managed Liverpool in numerous competitions, including the Premier League, UEFA Champions League, FA Cup, EFL Cup, and FIFA Club World Cup, among others. Playing over 470+ games.

- **Wins:** Klopp's emphasis on attacking football and gegenpressing is reflected in Liverpool's impressive win count. The team has secured victories in domestic and international competitions, showcasing Klopp's ability to adapt his tactics across different platforms. He holds his head high with a percentage of over 60% wins across 470+ games. He holds the the second longest unbeaten Premier League run of 44 games between January 2019 and February 2020, second to Arsene Wenger's Arsenal between May 2003 and October 2004.

- **Draws:** A balance between attacking flair and defensive stability is evident in the number of draws, reflecting the resilience of Klopp's teams in competitive fixtures.

- **Losses:** While Klopp's Liverpool has experienced setbacks, the number of losses is comparatively low, highlighting the team's consistency and ability to bounce back from defeats.

Premier League Records

The Premier League is the pinnacle of English football, and Klopp's impact has been profound in the domestic competition. Let's delve into some key statistics related to Liverpool's performance in the Premier League under Klopp.

- **Points Tally:** Klopp's Liverpool consistently accumulated high points totals, reflecting sustained excellence over the course of league campaigns. He holds the third highest point tally in EPL for coaches with over 100 games with a point of 2.11 per game in over 320 games.

- **Win Percentage:** Klopp boasts an impressive win percentage in the Premier League, underscoring

Liverpool's dominance in domestic fixtures. He has a winning percentage of over 65% in the premier league over 9 seasons.

- **Goals For and Against:** Klopp's attacking philosophy is evident in the high number of goals scored, while defensive solidity is reflected in the goals conceded column.

- **Clean Sheets:** The ability to keep clean sheets is crucial in league football. Klopp's Liverpool has showcased defensive resilience with a commendable number of clean sheets.

UEFA Champions League Records

The UEFA Champions League is the pinnacle of European club football, and Klopp's Liverpool etched its name in history with memorable campaigns. Let's explore some key statistics related to Liverpool's performance in the Champions League under Klopp.

- **Titles Won:** Klopp's crowning achievement in Europe is Liverpool's triumph in the UEFA Champions League. The number of titles won is a testament to the team's success on the continental stage.

List of trophies won by allopathic

- Premier League: 2019/20.
- FA Cup: 2021/22.
- EFL Cup: 2021/22.
- FA Community Shield: 2022.
- UEFA Champions League: 2018/19.
- UEFA Super Cup: 2019.

- FIFA Club World Cup: 2019.

- Final Appearances: Klopp guided Liverpool to multiple Champions League finals, showcasing a consistent ability to navigate the complexities of the knockout stages.

- Goals Scored: Liverpool's attacking prowess is reflected in the number of goals scored in the Champions League, with memorable performances etched in the memories of fans.

- Clean Sheets: Defensive solidity is crucial in knockout competitions, and Klopp's teams have demonstrated the ability to keep clean sheets in crucial European ties.

Team Achievements and Milestones

Beyond individual competitions, Klopp's Liverpool has achieved team-wide milestones that contribute to the overall narrative of success. Let's explore some of these noteworthy achievements.

- Longest Unbeaten Runs: Klopp's Liverpool embarked on remarkable unbeaten runs in various competitions, showcasing the team's ability to maintain consistency over an extended period. He has an unbeaten premier league run from January 2019 to February 2020 spanning over 44 games. He's just behind the mighty Arsenal invisible team of 2004.

- Historic Winning Streaks: Klopp's emphasis on relentless attacking play has led to historic winning streaks, setting records for consecutive victories in domestic and international competitions. In the premier league he shares the joint longest winning run with Guardiola's city of 18 consecutive premier league victories between October 2019 to February 2020.

- Goal-Scoring Feats: Liverpool, under Klopp, has achieved remarkable goal-scoring feats in individual matches, emphasizing the team's potency in the final third.

- Record Points Tally in Premier League: Klopp's Liverpool set a new standard for points accumulated in a Premier League season, surpassing previous records and showcasing the team's dominance. Liverpool's Klopp holds the second best point tally in the premier league of 99 points in the 2019/2020 season to win their first ever Premier League title.

Individual Player Achievements

While team achievements are pivotal, Klopp's Liverpool has also witnessed individual players reaching notable milestones under his guidance. Let's explore some of these individual player achievements.

- **Golden Boot Winners:** Klopp's attacking style has seen Liverpool players secure the Premier League Golden Boot for being the top goal-scorer in a season.

List of times Liverpool play won the Golden boot under Klopp

- M. Salah 2017/18 32 goals

- S. Mane & Salah 2018/19 22 goals
- S. Salah 2021/22 23 goals.

- **Assist Leaders:** The emphasis on team play and fluid attacking movements has contributed to Liverpool players leading the charts in terms of assists.

- **Player Awards:** Individual recognition, such as PFA Player of the Year, FWA Footballer of the Year, and other accolades, has been bestowed upon Liverpool players under Klopp's management.

Statistical Insights into Tactical Evolution

Beyond the traditional statistics, Klopp's tenure at Liverpool provides insights into the evolution of tactics and playing style. Statistical analysis can reveal patterns in possession, pressing intensity, passing accuracy, and other metrics that define Klopp's brand of football.

- **Possession Statistics:** Klopp's teams have showcased an ability to control possession, balancing proactive attacking play with defensive solidity.

- **Pressing Metrics:** Gegenpressing is a hallmark of Klopp's tactical philosophy, and statistical metrics related to pressing intensity and successful regains highlight Liverpool's effectiveness in disrupting opponents.

- **Passing Accuracy and Patterns:** The precision and creativity in Liverpool's passing, as reflected in passing accuracy and key pass metrics, provide insights into the team's ability to unlock opposition defenses.

- Shot Conversion Rates:

Klopp's emphasis on creating high-quality goal-scoring opportunities is evident in shot conversion rates, showcasing the team's clinical finishing. Jürgen Klopp's managerial records at Liverpool form a rich tapestry woven with victories, milestones, and statistical achievements. From domestic dominance in the Premier League to European glory in the Champions League, Klopp's impact transcends mere numbers. It's a story of attacking brilliance, defensive resilience, and a collective ethos that has redefined Liverpool's identity in the footballing landscape.

Chapter Seven: Legacy and Impact: Jürgen Klopp's Enduring Influence on Liverpool

Introduction: Crafting a Legacy Beyond Trophies

Jürgen Klopp's legacy at Liverpool extends far beyond the silverware he has lifted. It's a tale of transformation, resilience, and the rekindling of a footballing spirit that has left an indelible mark on Liverpool Football Club. As we delve into the legacy and impact of Klopp, it's essential to explore the various facets that contribute to the enduring influence he has imprinted on the club.

1. Cultural Renaissance: "Heavy Metal Football" and Anfield Magic

Klopp's arrival ushered in a cultural renaissance at Liverpool, epitomized by the vibrant style of play dubbed "Heavy Metal Football." The high-intensity pressing, dynamic attacking play, and the emotional charge on the touchline became synonymous with Klopp's era. Anfield, under Klopp's guidance, witnessed magical nights and historic comebacks, creating an atmosphere that resonated with fans and opponents alike. Klopp's impact on the cultural identity of Liverpool is evident not just in victories but in the passionate and exhilarating brand of football that has become a hallmark of the club.

2. Unity and Camaraderie: "The Klopp Effect" in the Dressing Room

Klopp's ability to foster unity and camaraderie within the squad is often referred to as "The Klopp Effect." The sense of togetherness, the emphasis on collective celebration, and the genuine joy shared among players have created a harmonious dressing room environment. This unity is not just a byproduct of success but a deliberate aspect of Klopp's man-management style. The bond between players extends beyond the pitch, creating a family-like atmosphere that has contributed to the team's success and resilience in challenging moments.

3. Player Development: Nurturing Talents and Elevating Careers

Klopp's commitment to player development is evident in the

emergence of young talents and the elevated performances of established stars. The integration of academy players like Trent Alexander-Arnold and Curtis Jones into the first team showcases Klopp's belief in nurturing homegrown talent. Additionally, Klopp has played a pivotal role in revitalizing and elevating the careers of certain players who have flourished under his guidance. The emphasis on holistic player development extends beyond tactical roles to instill a sense of responsibility and confidence in each player.

4. Mental Resilience and "Heavy Metal" Mentality

The mental resilience instilled by Klopp has been a defining characteristic of

Liverpool's success. The ability to bounce back from setbacks, late goals, and challenging periods is a testament to the "Heavy Metal" mentality that Klopp has cultivated. This mental fortitude has been crucial in achieving comebacks, securing crucial victories, and navigating the pressures of high-stakes competitions. Klopp's motivational skills and positive reinforcement contribute to a winning mindset that permeates the entire squad.

5. Global Impact and Fan Engagement

Klopp's charismatic personality and the entertaining style of play have propelled Liverpool into a global phenomenon. The club's fanbase has expanded, with supporters from diverse corners of the world uniting under the banner of Liverpool FC. Klopp's press conferences, interviews, and touchline antics have become iconic, contributing to the club's global appeal. Beyond the football pitch, Klopp's involvement in charitable initiatives and social responsibility projects has further endeared him to fans, creating a positive impact that extends beyond the realms of sport.

6. Redefining Anfield's Aura: The Klopp Era's Anfield

Anfield, under Klopp's management, has experienced a renaissance that goes beyond the physical confines of the stadium. The iconic "You'll Never Walk Alone" anthem reverberates with added fervor, creating an electric atmosphere on matchdays. The famous European nights, highlighted by comebacks and thrilling victories, have become part of Anfield's folklore. Klopp's impact is etched into the very fabric of the stadium, transforming it into a fortress where dreams are realized and memories are eternally imprinted.

7. The Klopp Philosophy: Gegenpressing and Footballing Identity

Gegenpressing, Klopp's tactical philosophy, has not only brought success on the pitch but has also defined Liverpool's footballing identity. The commitment to high-intensity pressing, rapid transitions, and entertaining football has left an imprint on the club's DNA. Even beyond Klopp's tenure, the influence of his tactical principles is likely to endure, shaping the way future Liverpool teams approach the beautiful game. Klopp's philosophy is not merely a tactical strategy; it's a legacy that has become intertwined with the essence of Liverpool's playing style.

8. Overcoming Setbacks: The Journey to Triumph

Klopp's legacy is not just about the triumphs but also the journey that saw Liverpool overcome setbacks and challenges. The near misses, the lessons learned from difficult seasons, and the process of rebuilding have contributed to the resilience ingrained in Klopp's teams. The ability to learn, adapt, and persevere in the face of adversity has become a defining characteristic of Klopp's Liverpool, showcasing a determination that mirrors the manager's own journey. Jürgen Klopp's legacy and impact on Liverpool extend beyond the realms of conventional success. It's a story of cultural revival, unity, player development, mental resilience, global influence, and a footballing philosophy that has redefined the club's identity. Klopp's imprint on Liverpool's soul is not measured solely in trophies but in the intangible elements that have rejuvenated the spirit of the club and its supporters. As the Klopp era continues to unfold, the legacy crafted by the German maestro remains a testament to the transformative power of football and the enduring bond between a manager, a team, and a passionate fanbase.

The Transformation of Culture and Identity: Klopp's Enduring Impact on Liverpool

Introduction: Redefining the Essence

Jürgen Klopp's tenure at Liverpool has not only been about victories on the pitch but a profound transformation of the club's culture and identity. From the vibrant style of play to the unity within the squad, Klopp has redefined what it means to be part of Liverpool Football Club. In this exploration, we delve into the key aspects of how Klopp has shaped and transformed the very essence of Liverpool.

1. High-Octane Football and "Heavy Metal" Philosophy

One of the most striking transformations under Klopp has been the style of play. The introduction of "Heavy Metal Football," characterized by intense pressing, dynamic attacks, and rapid transitions, has become the defining identity of Liverpool. The high-octane style not only brings success but also resonates with fans worldwide, creating an exhilarating brand of football that has reinvigorated the club's ethos.

2. Embracing Anfield's Magic: The Klopp Effect

Anfield, under Klopp, has experienced a renaissance. The famous stadium has not just been a venue for matches but a theater of dreams where extraordinary moments unfold. The emotional charge on the touchline, the fervent support of the fans, and the iconic rendition of "You'll Never Walk Alone" have become integral to Anfield's magic. Klopp's ability to harness the power of the crowd has transformed the stadium into a fortress where dreams are realized and victories are celebrated with unwavering passion.

3. Unity and Camaraderie: The Klopp Brotherhood

Klopp's emphasis on unity and camaraderie within the squad has birthed the concept of the "Klopp Brotherhood." The sense of togetherness extends beyond the pitch, creating a tight-knit group that celebrates successes collectively and faces challenges as one. This unity has not only fortified the team during difficult moments but has also created a positive environment that fosters player development and resilience.

4. From Doubters to Believers: Klopp's Inspirational Mantra

Klopp's arrival saw a shift in mentality, encapsulated by the famous phrase "From Doubters to Believers." This mantra has become a rallying cry for players and fans alike, symbolizing the transformation in mindset. The belief in overcoming odds, the resilience to bounce back from setbacks, and the unwavering determination to pursue success have become embedded in the club's ethos, shaping a narrative of triumph over adversity.

5. Player Development and the Klopp Effect

Klopp's impact extends to player development, transforming promising talents into key figures. The rise of academy players like Trent Alexander-Arnold and the rejuvenation of established stars exemplify Klopp's knack for nurturing talent. The emphasis on holistic player development goes beyond tactical roles, instilling a sense of responsibility, confidence, and belonging within each player.

6. Global Reach and Liverpool's Resurgence

Under Klopp, Liverpool's influence has transcended geographical boundaries. The club's global reach has expanded exponentially, with fans from diverse backgrounds uniting in their support. Klopp's charismatic personality, entertaining style of play, and engaging interviews have contributed to Liverpool's resurgence as a global footballing force. The impact extends beyond victories, creating a sense of community and belonging for fans worldwide.

7. Thriving in Adversity: Klopp's Leadership During Challenges

Klopp's transformative leadership is evident in how the team thrives in adversity. Whether overcoming injuries, navigating challenging fixtures, or facing setbacks, Klopp has instilled a resilient spirit within the squad. The ability to maintain high performance levels during difficult periods reflects not just tactical acumen but a mental fortitude that defines Klopp's brand of football.

A look into Liverpool's history, Klopp has woven a cultural narrative that extends beyond football. The club's identity has been revitalized, and a new era has emerged where success is not just measured in trophies but in the intangible elements that define a footballing culture. Klopp's transformative impact on Liverpool's culture and identity is a testament to the enduring power of leadership, belief, and the ability to forge a collective spirit that transcends the boundaries of the beautiful game. As Liverpool continues its journey, Klopp's legacy will remain embedded in the very fabric of the club, shaping its identity for years to come.

Chapter Eight: Life After Liverpool: Jürgen Klopp's Legacy and Future Endeavors

Introduction: The Decision to Step Down

Jürgen Klopp's announcement of stepping down as the manager of Liverpool sent shockwaves through the footballing world. His decision to leave a club where he achieved historic triumphs and forged an unbreakable bond with players and fans marked the end of a remarkable era. In this exploration, we delve into Klopp's reflections on his time at Liverpool, the factors behind his decision to step down, and the speculations surrounding his future endeavors.

1. Reflecting on a Glorious Journey

As Klopp bids farewell to Liverpool, it's essential to reflect on the journey that brought unprecedented success to Anfield. From his arrival in October 2015 to leading Liverpool to their first league title in 30 years, Klopp's time at the club has been a saga of highs, lows, and transformative moments. Reflecting on this journey, Klopp has shared insights into the emotional rollercoaster, the joyous celebrations, and the challenges that defined his tenure.

Triumphs and Trophies:

Klopp's tenure saw Liverpool claim major trophies, including the UEFA Champions League and the Premier League. The iconic moments, the historic comebacks, and the outpouring of emotion after each triumph have left an indelible mark on Klopp's legacy.

Challenges and Setbacks:

The journey was not without its challenges. Klopp faced seasons where Liverpool narrowly missed out on titles, experienced injuries to key players, and navigated periods of rebuilding. These challenges, while testing, contributed to the resilience and character that defined Klopp's Liverpool.

Player Relationships and Squad Unity:

One of Klopp's strengths has been his ability to form deep connections with his players. The squad's unity, the camaraderie within the dressing room, and the mutual respect between Klopp and his players have been pivotal in

Liverpool's success. Klopp's reflections likely include the profound impact these relationships have had on the team's dynamics.

The Decision to Step Down: Running Out of Energy

Klopp's announcement of stepping down was accompanied by a candid acknowledgment that he is "running out of energy." The decision, made known to the club in November, stunned many, considering Klopp's earlier commitment to continuing until 2026. Exploring the factors behind this decision reveals a complex interplay of personal considerations, the demanding nature of elite football management, and Klopp's unwavering commitment to giving his all to the role.

Physical and Mental Toll:

The role of a football manager at a top-tier club is physically and mentally demanding. Klopp, known for his passionate touchline presence and hands-on approach, has acknowledged that the constant pressure and responsibility took a toll on his energy levels. The emotional investment required to lead a team to glory, coupled with the challenges faced in the previous season, contributed to Klopp's decision to take a break.

A Season of Rebuilding:

The 2020-2021 season was a challenging one for Liverpool. The team faced injuries to key players, experienced a dip in form, and finished fifth in the Premier League. Klopp described the season as "difficult," highlighting the need for rebuilding. The subsequent summer saw Liverpool make strategic signings and adjustments to the squad, but the process of rejuvenation may have contributed to Klopp's recognition of the need for a pause.

Managerial Style and Energy Levels:

Klopp's managerial style is characterized by high-energy pressing, relentless attacking play, and a hands-on approach to coaching. This style, while immensely effective, requires significant energy and passion. Klopp's acknowledgment that he cannot continue in the same manner suggests a deep self-awareness about the nature of his managerial approach and the energy it demands.

Speculations and Plans for the Future

Klopp's announcement inevitably sparked speculations about his future plans. While the immediate focus is on taking a break from managerial responsibilities, Klopp's stature and track record ensure that he will be a sought-after figure in the footballing world. Exploring the speculations and potential future endeavors sheds light on the myriad possibilities that lie ahead for the German tactician.

Sabbatical or New Challenge:

It's not uncommon for managers to take a sabbatical after an intense managerial stint. Klopp himself took a brief break before joining Liverpool. Speculation abounds about whether Klopp will opt for a period of rest and reflection or if a new challenge awaits him. The allure of a sabbatical provides an opportunity for Klopp to recharge and assess his next move.

International Management:

One of the speculated paths for Klopp's future is international management. The prospect of leading a national team, perhaps even his native Germany, has been discussed. Klopp's tactical acumen, man-management skills, and experience at the highest level make him an attractive candidate for international football. The timing of major international tournaments coincides with Klopp's availability, adding intrigue to this speculation.

Club Management:

While Klopp has emphasized the need for a break, the allure of club management remains a possibility. Top clubs across Europe may express interest in securing Klopp's services when he decides to return to the managerial hot seat. The prospect of seeing Klopp bring his brand of football to a new club adds an element of anticipation to the post-Liverpool chapter of his career.

Media and Advisory Roles:

Beyond the touchline, Klopp's charisma and footballing insights could make him a compelling figure in the media. The transition to punditry, analysis, or advisory roles is a common trajectory for esteemed managers. Klopp's ability to articulate his views, combined with his deep understanding of the game, positions him as a potential media personality or advisor to footballing organizations.

A Pivotal Moment in Klopp's Journey

As Jürgen Klopp navigates the transition from Liverpool, the decision to step down marks a pivotal moment in his illustrious managerial journey. Reflecting on a journey that brought glory to Anfield, Klopp's decision to recharge and reassess his future opens the door to a myriad of possibilities. Whether a sabbatical, international management, a return to club football, or a venture into media and advisory roles, Klopp's post-Liverpool chapter will be closely watched by the footballing world. As the speculation continues, one thing is certain – Klopp's impact on football extends beyond a single club, and the next chapter in his storied career promises to be as intriguing as the legacy he leaves behind at Liverpool.

Chapter Nine:Tactical Insights: Unraveling Klopp's Mastery at Liverpool

Jürgen Klopp's time at Liverpool has been synonymous with a distinctive brand of football that combines high-intensity pressing, dynamic attacking play, and a relentless pursuit of success. In this exploration, we delve into the tactical innovations that defined Klopp's tenure at Liverpool, unraveling the intricacies of his strategic approach and examining the specific strategies employed during crucial matches that shaped the club's glorious journey.

Gegenpressing: The Engine of Klopp's Play

At the heart of Klopp's tactical philosophy is the concept of gegenpressing – a system that prioritizes immediate ball recovery after losing possession. Gegenpressing is not merely a defensive strategy; it's a proactive method to disrupt opponents and regain control quickly. Klopp's Liverpool became renowned for its efficiency in executing gegenpressing, creating turnovers high up the pitch and launching rapid counter-attacks.

Intensity and Coordination:

The success of gegenpressing lies in the collective intensity and coordination of the entire team. Klopp's players were drilled to swarm the opposition, pressuring them into mistakes and limiting their options. The synchronized pressing movements were a hallmark of Klopp's tactical blueprint, creating chaos for opponents attempting to play out from the back.

Transition Moments:
Gegenpressing is most effective during transition moments – immediately after losing possession. Klopp's Liverpool mastered the art of winning the ball back within seconds of conceding, catching opponents off guard and exploiting the disorganization that follows turnovers. This tactical emphasis on swift transitions contributed to Liverpool's reputation as a devastating counter-attacking force.

Dynamic Front Three: Fluidity in Attack

Klopp's attacking trio, often comprising players like Mohamed Salah, Sadio Mané, and Roberto Firmino, exemplified fluidity and interchangeability. The front three operated as a cohesive unit, constantly interchanging positions to disorient defenses. Salah, Mané, and Firmino's ability to operate in various attacking roles added an unpredictable dimension to Liverpool's play.

Inside Forwards and False Nine:

While Salah and Mané predominantly played as wide forwards, their tactical roles evolved throughout matches. The inside forward positions allowed them to cut inside onto their stronger foot, posing a goal threat. Firmino, often deployed as a false nine, created space for the wide forwards by dropping deeper and engaging defenders, contributing to Liverpool's intricate attacking patterns.

Pressing from the Front:

Beyond goal-scoring prowess, the front three played a crucial role in Klopp's gegenpressing system. Their relentless pressing from the front set the tone for the entire team, disrupting opposition build-up and forcing errors. This defensive contribution from attacking players was integral to Klopp's tactical framework.

Full-Backs: Engine of Width and Creativity

Klopp's tactical setup emphasized the importance of full-backs as key contributors to both defensive solidity and attacking width. Full-backs like Trent Alexander-Arnold and Andrew Robertson played pivotal roles in stretching opposition defenses, providing width in attack, and delivering precise crosses into the box.

Attacking Overloads:

Klopp encouraged his full-backs to overlap and join the attack, creating numerical overloads in wide areas. This not only stretched opposing defenses horizontally but also allowed the full-backs to deliver dangerous crosses into the penalty area. The attacking prowess of Alexander-Arnold and Robertson contributed significantly to Liverpool's goal-scoring threat.

Defensive Versatility:

While known for their attacking contributions, Liverpool's full-backs also showcased defensive versatility. They were tasked with tracking back quickly during defensive transitions, ensuring defensive solidity when the team lost possession. This dual role demonstrated Klopp's emphasis on all-round contributions from every position on the pitch.

Set-Piece Mastery: A Tactical Weapon

Liverpool, under Klopp, became renowned for its proficiency in set-piece situations – both offensively and defensively. Klopp's meticulous planning and strategic setups for set-pieces turned these moments into potent weapons for the team.

Attacking Set-Pieces:
Liverpool's attacking set-pieces were characterized by well-drilled routines and inventive plays. Klopp's emphasis on creating mismatches and exploiting defensive vulnerabilities resulted in numerous goals from corners and free-kicks. The movement and positioning of key players during set-pieces were integral to their success.

Defensive Organization:
Defensively, Klopp instilled a disciplined and organized approach to set-pieces. The zonal marking system, coupled with

effective communication and clear roles for players, minimized the risk of conceding from dead-ball situations. Defensive solidity in set-pieces was an essential component of Klopp's overall tactical strategy.

Strategies in Crucial Matches: Iconic Moments

Klopp's tactical acumen shone brightest in crucial matches, where the strategic approach often played a decisive role in securing victories. Examining some iconic moments provides insights into Klopp's adaptability and tactical intelligence during pivotal encounters.

Champions League Final 2019 - Liverpool vs. Tottenham:

In the 2019 Champions League Final, Klopp's approach was pragmatic. Liverpool took an early lead through a Mohamed Salah penalty but faced a resilient Tottenham side. Klopp adjusted the team's approach, prioritizing defensive stability while maintaining a threat on the counter-attack. The 2-0 victory showcased Klopp's tactical flexibility in high-stakes matches.

Barcelona Comeback - Champions League Semifinal 2018-19:

Down 3-0 after the first leg of the semifinal against Barcelona, Klopp orchestrated one of the greatest comebacks in Champions League history. Klopp's tactical adjustments included a high defensive line, quick transitions, and exploiting set-piece opportunities. The 4-0 triumph demonstrated Klopp's ability to inspire tactical resilience and exploit opponents' weaknesses.

Premier League Title Decider - Liverpool vs. Manchester City 2018-19:

In a crucial Premier League encounter against Manchester City, Klopp's tactical approach was measured. Liverpool secured a 3-1 victory, with Klopp's emphasis on defensive solidity evident. The team absorbed City's attacks and capitalized on counter-attacks, showcasing Klopp's strategic nous in key league fixtures.

Jürgen Klopp's tactical innovations at Liverpool have left an indelible mark on the footballing landscape. From gegenpressing to the dynamic front three, Klopp's strategies were both innovative and effective. The mastery in set-pieces and adaptability in crucial matches showcased Klopp's tactical intelligence. As Klopp takes a break from managerial duties, his tactical legacy at Liverpool remains a blueprint for success, influencing managers and teams worldwide. Klopp's impact goes beyond trophies; it's a tactical legacy that has redefined modern football and will continue to inspire the next generation of coaches.

Chapter Ten: Klopp-Fan Relationship: A Symphony of Passion and Adoration

Jürgen Klopp's tenure at Liverpool has been more than a mere managerial stint; it's been a deeply emotional and symbiotic relationship with the club's supporters. In this exploration, we delve into the unique bond between Klopp and the Liverpool fans, examining the famous "pump celebration" that has become an iconic symbol of their shared passion. Through reflections from Liverpool supporters, we uncover the profound impact of Klopp's era on the hearts and souls of those who call themselves the "Reds."

The Pump Celebration: A Symbol of Unity

The image is etched in the minds of Liverpool fans worldwide – Jürgen Klopp, fists pumping the air, heart pounding with unbridled joy. The "pump celebration" has become a symbol of triumph, resilience, and shared ecstasy. Exploring the roots of this iconic celebration unveils the emotional connection that Klopp forged with the Anfield faithful.

Spontaneity and Authenticity:

The beauty of Klopp's pump celebration lies in its spontaneity and authenticity. Whether celebrating a crucial goal or a historic triumph, Klopp's unfiltered emotions manifest in this visceral display of passion. The celebration is not a choreographed routine; it's a genuine expression of the intense connection between Klopp, the players, and the fans.

Shared Joy in Victories:

The pump celebration is often associated with moments of victory – be it a last-minute winner, a crucial goal in a title race, or a triumph in a major final. Klopp's jubilation mirrors the collective joy of Liverpool supporters, creating a shared emotional experience that transcends the boundaries between the manager and the fans.

Cultural Iconography:

Beyond its emotional resonance, the pump celebration has become a cultural icon within the broader context of football celebrations. Klopp's exuberance reflects the unbridled passion that defines the beautiful game, resonating with fans of various clubs and even those with no specific allegiance. The celebration symbolizes the essence of football – raw emotion, shared ecstasy, and the pursuit of glory.

Klopp's Connection with the Anfield Faithful

Klopp's relationship with Liverpool supporters extends far beyond the celebratory moments on the touchline. It's a connection forged through shared values, a mutual understanding of the club's ethos, and a genuine appreciation for the role fans play in the success of the team.

Understanding the Culture:

From day one, Klopp demonstrated a profound understanding of Liverpool's unique footballing culture. His embrace of the club's history, the significance of Anfield, and the fervent loyalty of the supporters endeared him to the fanbase. Klopp's ability to connect with the cultural fabric of Liverpool laid the foundation for a relationship built on mutual respect and shared passion.

Inclusion and Unity:

Klopp's "inclusive football" philosophy extends beyond the pitch to include the fans as integral members of the Liverpool family. He has consistently emphasized the importance of unity, with the fans playing a crucial role in creating the electric atmosphere at Anfield. Klopp's acknowledgment of the fans as the "12th man" reinforces the idea that success is a collective endeavor.

Embracing the Community:

Klopp's connection with Liverpool fans goes beyond matchdays. His involvement in community initiatives, charitable work, and genuine interactions with supporters create a sense of belonging. Whether it's visiting local schools, engaging in charity events, or connecting with fans through various channels, Klopp has become not just a manager but a beloved figure within the broader Liverpool community.

Reflections from Liverpool Supporters

Liverpool supporters, often referred to as the "Reds," have experienced a rollercoaster of emotions during Klopp's era – from the exhilaration of historic triumphs to the shared resilience in challenging moments. Through their reflections, we gain insights into the profound impact Klopp has had on the emotional landscape of Liverpool fandom.

"He Gets Us":

One recurring sentiment among Liverpool supporters is the feeling that Klopp truly understands the fans. His passion, authenticity, and unwavering commitment mirror the emotions of supporters who have lived through the highs and lows of supporting the club. The shared sense of identity creates a bond that goes beyond the traditional manager-fan relationship.

Collective Ecstasy in Victories:

The moments of triumph under Klopp have been defining chapters in the collective memory of Liverpool supporters. Whether it's the Champions League triumph in 2019, the long-awaited Premier League title in 2020, or dramatic comebacks in crucial matches, Klopp's celebrations resonate with the joyous outpouring of emotions from fans worldwide. The shared ecstasy in victories creates lasting memories that bind Klopp and the supporters together.

Emotional Anchoring in Setbacks:

In moments of setbacks and challenges, Klopp's demeanor and words have served as emotional anchors for Liverpool supporters. The manager's ability to articulate the feelings of disappointment, offer reassurance, and maintain a positive outlook has provided solace to fans during difficult periods. Klopp's empathy and understanding of the emotional investment fans have in the club contribute to a sense of shared resilience.

Cultural Revival at Anfield:

Klopp's impact on the culture of Anfield has been transformative. The famous anthem "You'll Never Walk Alone" reverberates with heightened passion, the stadium becomes a cauldron of emotion, and the collective roar of the fans amplifies the team's performance. The cultural revival under Klopp is not just about victories but the emotional reawakening of Anfield as a fortress of fervent support.

As Jürgen Klopp's era at Liverpool unfolds, the relationship between the manager and the supporters emerges as a symphony of passion, unity, and shared emotions. The pump celebration, a spontaneous manifestation of Klopp's joy, becomes a visual anthem for the collective heartbeat of Anfield. Through the reflections of Liverpool supporters, it's evident that Klopp's impact goes beyond tactical brilliance and silverware – it's etched in the emotional landscape of the fans who have found a kindred spirit in their charismatic manager.

Klopp's era is not just a chapter in Liverpool's history; it's a love affair that transcends the boundaries of football, leaving an indelible mark in the hearts of the Reds.

Conclusion: Jürgen Klopp's Enduring Legacy at Liverpool

Summary of Klopp's Legacy

Jürgen Klopp's tenure at Liverpool transcends the realms of mere managerial success – it is a saga of passion, resilience, and transformative brilliance that has left an indelible mark on the fabric of the club. As we reflect on Klopp's legacy, several key facets encapsulate the essence of his impact at Liverpool.

1. Trophies and Triumphs:

Klopp's era at Liverpool witnessed a trophy haul that quenched the thirst of Reds fans for silverware. The iconic

Champions League triumph in 2019, followed by the long-awaited Premier League title in 2020, etched Klopp's name in Liverpool's storied history. His ability to lead the team to glory in major competitions rejuvenated the trophy cabinet and fulfilled the dreams of an entire fanbase.

2. Tactical Revolution:

Klopp's tactical innovations, epitomized by the gegenpressing philosophy and dynamic attacking play, revolutionized Liverpool's style of football. The high-octane, relentless approach not only brought success but also became a blueprint for modern football. Klopp's influence extended beyond Anfield, shaping the tactical landscape of the sport.

3. Cultural Renaissance:

Anfield, under Klopp, experienced a cultural renaissance. The famous anthem "You'll Never Walk Alone" resonated with newfound passion, the stadium became a fortress of unwavering support, and the connection between players, manager, and fans reached unprecedented levels. Klopp's emphasis on unity, inclusivity, and understanding of Liverpool's unique footballing culture revived the soul of the club.

4. Emotional Symphony:

The pump celebration, eternally linked with Klopp's moments of unbridled joy, became a visual anthem for the emotional symphony shared between the manager and the Liverpool faithful.

The genuine, spontaneous expression of emotion on the touchline mirrored the collective heartbeat of Anfield, creating iconic images that define an era.

Final Thoughts on Klopp's Impact

Jürgen Klopp's impact on Liverpool and football as a whole extends far beyond the tangible achievements and records. His legacy is imprinted in the intangible elements that define the essence of the beautiful game.

1. Leadership and Unity:

Klopp's leadership extended beyond the tactical realm; it was about fostering unity and a sense of togetherness. His ability to create a "Klopp Brotherhood" within the squad, instilling belief and resilience, showcased the transformative power of inspirational leadership in football.

2. The Human Side of Management:

In an era where football can become dominated by metrics and data, Klopp's emphasis on the human side of management stood out. His authenticity, emotional intelligence, and genuine connection with players and fans highlighted the profound impact that personal relationships can have in the world of elite football.

3. Redefining Success:

Klopp's era at Liverpool redefined success not just in terms of trophies but in the emotional tapestry woven within the club. The "From Doubters to Believers" mantra encapsulates a shift in mindset that goes beyond the scoreboard – it's about overcoming challenges, believing in the impossible, and forging a collective identity that withstands the test of time.

4. A Blueprint for Inspiration:

Klopp's journey at Liverpool serves as a blueprint for inspiration. From rebuilding a squad to achieving historic triumphs, his resilience, passion, and commitment to a vision became a source of inspiration for managers, players, and fans worldwide. Klopp's impact is a testament to the enduring power of belief, unity, and the pursuit of excellence.

In Closing: Klopp's Chapter in Football History

As Jürgen Klopp steps away from the managerial helm at Liverpool, his chapter in football history becomes immortalized. It's a chapter defined not just by victories and titles but by the emotional tapestry woven with the threads of passion, unity, and a relentless pursuit of glory. Klopp's legacy extends beyond the touchline; it lives in the hearts of Liverpool supporters and serves as a guiding light for the next generation of football enthusiasts. The Klopp era was more than a managerial stint; it was a symphony of footballing brilliance that will echo through Anfield and reverberate in the annals of football history for generations to come.

Printed in Great Britain
by Amazon

45301570R00086